Page

Introduction   1

Section 1 – An Overview of Ship Vetting

1.1 Assessment Criteria   3

1.2 The Elements of Vetting   3

    1.2.1 Ship/Shore Compatibility 3

    1.2.2 Assessing Ship Quality 3

    1.2.3 Assessment for Use 7

1.3 The Advantages and Benefits of Vetting   8

Section 2 – Application of Vetting in an LNG Context   9

2.1 Quality Assurance   9

2.2 Personnel   9

2.3 Ship/Shore Compatibility   9

2.4 Transparency   10

2.5 Flexibility and Availability   10

2.6 Inspections and SIRE   11

2.7 Age   11

2.8 Clearances   12

Section 3 – Specific Advice and Recommendations   13

3.1 To Inspectors and Inspection Companies   13

3.2 To Vetting Departments   13

3.3 To LNG Charterers, Brokers and Commercial Operators   13

3.4 To LNG Ship Managers/Owners/Pool Operators   14

3.5 To Ship's Staff   14

3.6 To LNG Terminal Operators   14

3.7 To Ship's Agents   15

References   17

Bibliography   19

Appendices   20

Glossary   33

Acknowledgements

SIGTTO would like to thank the following organisations for providing material which has been used in this document.

The Oil Companies International Marine Forum (OCIMF)

The International Association of Independent Tanker Owners (Intertanko)

Purpose and Scope

Inspection and vetting by charterers, buyers, terminal operators and sellers have been an integral part of ship operations in oil tanker and LPG carrier operations for over 25 years and have helped to improve operating standards over this period. The LNG trade has not been exposed to vetting because ships have tended to operate under long term contractual arrangements in dedicated trades between dedicated terminals.

Between the commencement of shipments in 1959 and the end of 2002, 3.23 billion m^3 of LNG had been shipped across the world without an incident resulting in loss of containment.

Recent changes in trading patterns have resulted in a number of short-term freight contracts, involving vessels trading to ports at which they have never previously called. Consequently, charterers, buyers, terminal operators and sellers need to assure themselves that the condition, operation and ownership of any vessel used are of an acceptable standard, by applying their ship inspection and vetting systems to LNG shipping.

This document draws on the lessons learned from the oil industry and provides information to all parties concerned with the vetting of LNG ships.
It is hoped that this will help to reduce any uncertainty and provide a smooth transition for LNG shipping into vetting.

Within this document, there are some references to the practices of individual companies. Such examples are given for guidance and may not reflect unanimous application by all industry members.

The Need to Vet Ships

Incidents such as pollution, fire, grounding and collision, can have potentially serious consequences for owners, managers, charterers, cargo owners and other involved parties. The responsibility for the safety management and quality of a ship rests ultimately with its owner through its technical operator. However charterers, buyers, terminal operators and sellers are exposed to certain risks when they use a third party vessel. The implications of death or injury to personnel, clean-up, asset loss, compensation and brand reputation have led charterers, cargo owners, loading and receiving facilities and other stakeholders to take measures to assure themselves that vessels used are of an appropriate standard.

Vetting of the quality of marine transportation equipment is a structured evaluation process that has been adopted and developed by organisations. Vetting departments aim to evaluate ship quality and to provide marine quality assurance to their principals.

This evaluation process has evolved over time within various organisations. Systems and processes vary due to company size, scope and diversity of marine activities (oil, chemical, LPG, LNG etc) attitude to marine risk and marine expertise employed. Each company will have its own acceptance criteria. Vessel selection and use is solely at each company's discretion.

During the period of use, the overall evaluation will generally be based upon a combination of the *likelihood* of an incident and the *consequences* to the user.

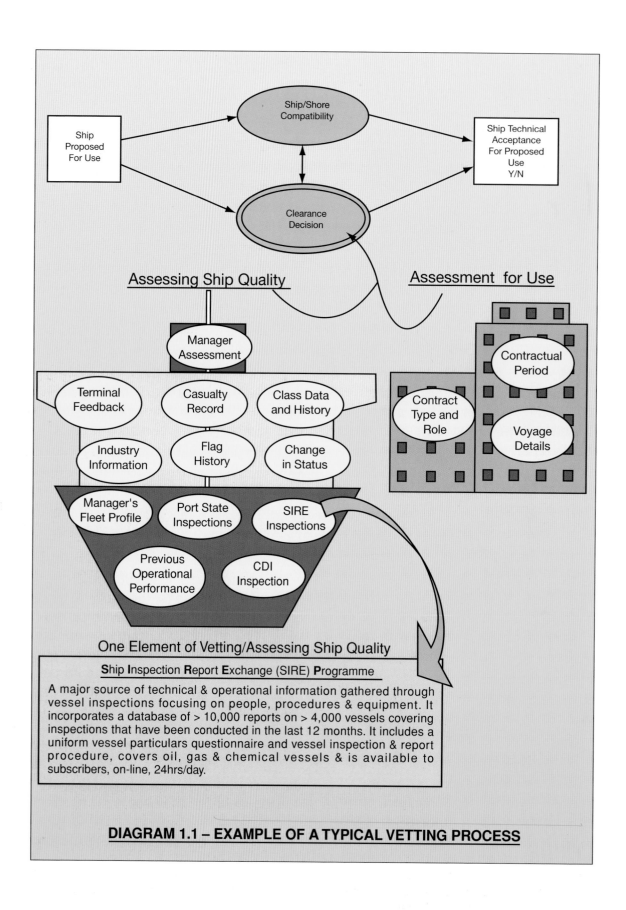

DIAGRAM 1.1 – EXAMPLE OF A TYPICAL VETTING PROCESS

1 An Overview of Ship Vetting

1.1 Assessment Criteria

Quality of vessels and their operation is assessed for compliance with international legislation, such as the Safety of *Life at Sea Convention (SOLAS)[11]*, and the *International Management Code for the Safe Operation of Ships* and for Pollution Prevention - the *International Safety Management (ISM) Code[12]*, and compliance with accepted industry standards, such as *Liquefied Gas Handling Principles (SIGTTO)[7]*, *The Tanker Safety Guide (Liquefied Gas) (ICS)[8]*, and *The International Safety Guide for Oil Tankers* and *Terminals (OCIMF/ICS/IAPH)[6]* etc.

Additional criteria may be applied by individual organisations.

1.2 The Elements of Vetting

The three key elements of vetting are:

- Ship/shore compatibility,
- Assessing ship quality, and
- Assessment for use.

These elements are illustrated in Diagram 1.1, and explained below.

1.2.1 Ship/Shore Compatibility

Different company organisational structures mean that the ship compatibility issue may be handled by the vetting department or by a different part of the organisation. This process will include evaluation of such factors as local or national regulations, ship dimensions versus any terminal limitations, cargo and mooring equipment, also climate and weather. Some oil majors maintain their own databases which incorporates terminal/port exclusion or restriction information about vessels used by them on a regular basis.

1.2.2 Assessing Ship Quality

The factors that govern the likelihood of an incident will be such items as the vessel's physical condition, the capabilities of the managing company, the vessel's history (in respect of inspection, casualty, operational efficiency, and frequency of flag, class, ownership, management changes and port state control detentions), the competence of the vessel's staff, the proposed ports and route, the ship type, any particular operation proposed, and the duration of the proposed contract.

Within vetting there are several decision processes. Most vetting departments employ marine professionals to make such decisions.

The term vetting encompasses the whole process of marine quality assurance evaluation. Vetting uses many tools and inspection is just one of these tools, as can be seen from Diagram 1.1.

Assessment of ship quality can include some or all of the following elements.

1.2.2.1 Ship Inspection

The principle purpose of a ship inspection is to provide a prospective user with factual and up to date information on such items as management, manning, safe operation, pollution prevention and cargo worthiness.

Vetting databases are populated from the many sources illustrated in Diagram 1.1. A key element of assessing ship quality is the evaluation of a ship inspection report. Such assessment may be based on SIRE, CDI, Terminal, or other inspection report types.

The system for inspection of vessels is handled differently by individual companies. Details on individual companies' systems are published and updated in the Intertanko booklet entitled *"A Guide to the Vetting Process"[2]*.

SIRE:

SIRE is a voluntary programme established in 1993 by OCIMF. The SIRE system is a very large database of up-to-date information about tankers. Essentially, SIRE has played a significant part in focusing tanker industry awareness on the importance of meeting satisfactory tanker quality and ship safety standards.

The SIRE inspection process is illustrated in activity sequence Diagram 1.2 below. This illustration is a broad outline, but inspecting companies may have additional processes for inspection agreements and for recovering inspection costs.

DIAGRAM 1.2 – ACTIVITY SEQUENCE DIAGRAM FOR A TYPICAL SIRE INSPECTION

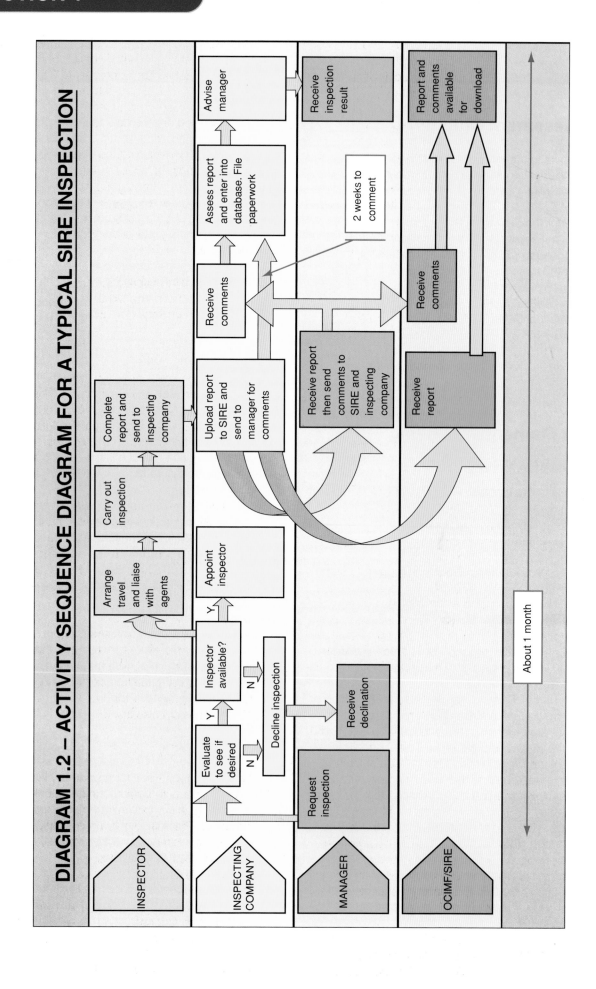

In order to ensure that an appointed inspector is appropriately experienced and qualified, OCIMF SIRE inspectors are subject to an accreditation procedure. This process is very detailed and takes into account the inspector's experience and qualifications. There is an examination and on-board training and audit process prior to accreditation, and systems for monitoring and periodic auditing are also in place.

Once an inspector has been accredited he will be issued with a certificate and a credit card sized photo identification, which will include details of the vessel types that the inspector is accredited to inspect.

It is important to recognise the role that an inspector plays in the overall vetting system. The objective of a SIRE inspection is to provide the ultimate user of a SIRE report with a factual record of the vessel's external condition and standard of operation at the time of the inspection. It is not a structural survey and does not involve inspection of internal cargo or void spaces as it is always carried out during cargo operations. This allows an assessment of the risks that use of the vessel might pose.

SIRE inspections utilise a document called the *Vessel Inspection Questionnaire* (VIQ) [1]. Inspectors must use this document in an inspection. (See Appendix 1)

It should be noted that the inspector is not usually empowered to make any decision regarding the use of the vessel, and must not include in any comment, any indication of ship acceptability or non acceptability (See Appendix 2). Any observations that the inspector intends to record should be pointed out and discussed on site at the time.

The ship owner/manager has a period of two weeks, from receiving the report, to respond to the observations before the report is released and made available to other OCIMF SIRE participants. The response will be read in conjunction with the report during the evaluation process. It should be noted that the manager's comments themselves also provide important information on the level of expertise and knowledge in the managing offices, and thus form an important contribution. The manager may also feedback to the inspecting company if he is unhappy about the conduct of an inspection.

SIRE database access is available, at a nominal cost, to OCIMF members, bulk oil terminal operators, port authorities, canal authorities and oil, power, industrial or oil trading companies which charter tankers as a normal part of their business. It is also available, free of charge, to Governmental bodies which supervise safety and/or pollution prevention in respect of oil tankers (e.g. port state control authorities, MOUs, etc).

The SIRE system also includes a *Harmonized Vessel Particulars Questionnaire (HVPQ)* element, which when completed gives information about ship particulars and required or customary documents which are of a permanent or semi-permanent nature, primarily related to safety and pollution prevention.

For more detailed information refer to Appendices 1-3: OCIMF, the Intertanko booklet [2], or the particular inspecting company.

CDI:

An alternative ship inspection system is run by the Chemical Distribution Institute (CDI). This system also produces inspection reports which are made available on line, and is designed for use in the inspection of chemical and gas carriers.

Terminal Feedback:

Terminals are an important link in the inspection activity chain, particularly in light of modern security requirements. Terminals need to be informed of impending inspections, and also need to be aware of the importance of inspections, so that inspectors can gain access to vessels.

Terminals may also provide feedback to their principals regarding a vessel's condition, operational performance or incidents experienced during a vessel call at the terminal. Where terminal representatives intend to make written observations to their principals, it is important that such observations are discussed on board at the time.

The Decision to Inspect:

When the need arises for an inspection the ship manager normally initiates the process by requesting an inspection from an inspecting company. The vetting department must then decide if the inspection will go ahead. When deciding whether to inspect, vetting departments may wish to take into account any or all of the following factors:

- the inspecting company's interest and priority for the vessel to be inspected.

- the availability of a suitably accredited inspector.

- the accessibility of the vessel, including the future schedule and trading pattern and the time of day. It is preferable to inspect many areas of the vessel during daylight.

- the amount of notice given.

- any recent changes of status of the ship (such as ownership, management, class or flag).

- the operation being conducted. For oil tankers a discharge port inspection is often preferred in order to see the vessel's cargo equipment in operation, and to verify the integrity of the cargo system. For LNG ships, cargo equipment is in operation during loading and discharging. In both cases this is an opportunity to observe the deck management team at work.

- the existence, age, quality and source of any earlier inspection reports.

The co-ordination of vessel and inspector movements requires planning and flexibility. Typically about 7-10 days notice is recommended for an inspection request, to facilitate demand assessment, although confirmation may not be received until nearer the time. The Intertanko booklet [2] gives some details regarding notice for individual companies.

1.2.2.2 Class Records

Classification Societies maintain records of the date and place of surveys, details of what was found, and the remedial action taken. All Classification Societies keep a record of defects that are outstanding and required to be rectified. These are defined as Conditions of Class. These records form an integral part of any ship vetting procedure. Class records, including steel thickness measurement records, may be examined during an inspection, and/or when vetting departments request Class documentation from the vessel's technical managers.

1.2.2.3 Port State Inspections

Port State Control is the process by which a nation exercises authority over foreign ships when those ships are in waters subject to its jurisdiction. The right to do this is derived from domestic law usually implementing international convention (treaty) obligations.

The purpose of Port State Control is to inspect foreign ships in national ports, to verify that the condition of the ship and its equipment complies with the requirements of applicable international conventions to which the state is a party and that the ship is manned and operated in compliance with these rules.

The OCIMF SIRE system is available, free of charge, to Port State Control authorities.

Port State Inspection databases may be used as part of the vetting process. Internet access to this data provides real time information on Port State vessel inspection findings and detentions. Any detentions or deficiencies noted may be reviewed and clarified with owners/managers as part of the vetting process.

1.2.2.4 Change in Status

Any change in a vessel's ownership, technical operator, manning agency, flag of registry, transfer of classification society etc. may be an indicator of a change in standards of management and operations. All changes in status should be scrutinised to determine the reasons for the change. Some changes may merit an inspection.

Flag History:

The frequency of flag changes, particularly if changes are concurrent with other changes in key management functions, should be routinely considered in vetting decisions, in gaining an overview of how the vessel is being operated.

Class History:

The frequency and reasons for a vessel's changes of Class, particularly where such changes are concurrent with other changes in status (Flag, owner, operator etc.) should be routinely considered in vetting decisions. Particular attention should be paid to those defects recorded by the losing Society and the method by which the correction of those defects is monitored and enforced under the new Classification Society.

Technical Manager:

If the vessel is under new technical management since the last inspection report, a new inspection may be required. Important elements for assessing quality when a vessel changes technical management, are changes to the vessel's manning and the implementation of a different Safety Management System (SMS).

1.2.2.5 Owner/Manager Assessment

Management Review:

A vetting department's review of a ship owner/manager's management systems, to assess its operational and technical competency. Where required these reviews may be carried out by inviting the technical managers to the offices of the vetting department, or by vetting department representatives visiting the technical manager's offices. They typically take a full day, and involve checks of the Safety Management Systems. After a review there is usually a period of follow-up correspondence and dialogue, after which an assessment of the managing company will be made. The assessment may also carry a period of validity.

Owner/Managers Fleet Profile:

The overall assessment of an owner/manager's fleet will provide a high level review of the standard of vessels being operated by a particular owner or manager. This assessment can be a key element in vetting decisions.

1.2.2.6 Structural Reviews

Structural review programmes based mainly on examination of Class documentation, may be carried out to evaluate the structural integrity of vessels. Depending upon the findings from the desktop reviews, it may be considered necessary to carry out onboard structural inspections. Some vetting departments may require a Condition Assessment Programme (CAP) rating for vessels of a certain type, age or size. Age alone is not an indicator of ship quality. Age is a factor which may be taken into account in the vetting process.

1.2.2.7 Casualty/Incidents

Casualty Records:

Records of a vessel's casualty history are available in the public domain. This may be sourced externally from service providers that track this information. Clarification from ship managers may be sought if deemed appropriate. Casualty information relating to other vessels of the same design or ownership may also affect vetting decisions.

Incidents:

When a vessel has been involved in an incident, potential users of the vessel may want to assure themselves that the incident has been properly investigated, and that appropriate corrective action has been taken. Much will depend on the nature of the incident. When vetting departments are asked to clear a vessel for use, they may not have anything other than brief details of the incident, and so may request information from the vessel's managers.

1.2.2.8 Previous Operational Performance

Operational performance, or charter feedback and/or terminal feedback, may be taken into consideration as part of the vetting process.

1.2.2.9 Industry Information

The data obtained from industry sources (publications, technical journals, industry committees and/or news media) may be reviewed and may form a part of the vetting process.

1.2.3 Assessment For Use

Prior to using a vessel the vetting process will also consider the implications of the proposed usage.

1.2.3.1 Clearances

One method of vetting is to use a **passive** system. With this approach, vessels are inspected and assessed periodically and, providing they are of an acceptable standard, they are approved for any use for a period of time. If nothing negative is received about the vessel, during the interim period between inspections, the vessel can still be used.

Alternatively, many vetting departments use an **active** system, whereby each time a vessel is offered, a freight trader (or similar person within an organisation) contacts the vetting department for a clearance to use that vessel. The vetting department uses its resources to seek information on the vessel, then makes a decision as to whether the vessel is considered acceptable for the business proposed, and notifies its decision to the freight trader.

This process also evaluates the **consequences** element. The basis of the sale and purchase agreement, the charter party, the type of cargo and the voyage details are combined with the quality assessment of the proposed vessel in order to arrive at a clearance decision. See Diagram 1.1

1.2.3.2 Longer Term Risks

Additional tools may be used where the proposed use, and hence exposure, is for a longer period, as in the case of time charters, contracts of affreightment, consecutive voyage charters, or simply for frequently used vessels/companies. Additional criteria may be applied before a vessel is accepted, such as Management Reviews of the managing company and/or a more intensive inspection regime. For example a vessel may have to undergo a pre-time charter inspection and subsequent periodic inspections. Some charterers may stipulate that any ship taken on time charter for a certain period will be re-inspected, at certain intervals, by their own representative. This is to ensure that certification and operating standards are maintained at the levels identified at the initial inspection and stipulated in the time charter. A SIRE report may or may not be produced after a time charter inspection.

1.2.3.3 New Buildings

Individual organisations may have specific policies regarding use of new vessels. Specific issues associated with new vessels (such as crew and management unfamiliarity, or un-proven systems and equipment) may require mitigation.

1.2.3.4 Terminal Acceptance

Terminal operators have a responsibility to manage safety at their facility. Most terminals retain the right to reject a vessel which is nominated to call at the terminal. In order that terminals can have confidence in the quality of vessels calling at their terminals, a system of quality assurance will normally be put in place. The principal's vetting system may constitute part of this process. Terminals may also independently subscribe to the SIRE system and download inspection reports.

1.3 The Advantages and Benefits of Vetting

The main purpose of vetting is marine quality assurance. There are several advantages and benefits which have resulted as this process has evolved.

Vetting systems in conjunction with Port State Control, the ISM Code and other industry initiatives, are leading to improvements in the quality and safety of ships and ship's staff.

Regular inspections help to maintain industry standards and safety awareness on board. An inspection provides a ship operator with an independent view of the operation of his vessel against these industry standards. This in turn can help to reduce port state control detentions and deficiencies.

The SIRE uniform vessel inspection procedure and inspector accreditation process ensures that factual inspection reports can be evaluated by users other than the inspecting company. This helps to reduce the number of inspections required and therefore the burden on ship's staff.

2 Application of Vetting in an LNG Context

2.1 Quality Assurance

In many cases, LNG ships are engaged on dedicated project trades. There can therefore be an in-depth understanding between project partners, terminals and individual ships. However, when LNG ships are engaged on short-term charters, diversions or swaps the prospective users do not have the benefit of this understanding. They will tend to use their vetting systems to gain comfort that industry regulations and guidelines are being complied with aboard the vessel, and that the risk of using the vessel has been minimised.

The LNG business has changed dramatically over the last few years. Charterers, buyers, terminal operators and sellers, require assurance that the ships being used are of adequate quality, and the quality assessment tool they commonly use is vetting. Operators of LNG ships must be cognisant of charterers', buyers', terminal operators' and sellers' needs, and respond accordingly. This response should include the actions recommended in Section 3.4.

2.2 Personnel

The existing long term, project nature of the LNG trade means that the individuals involved in LNG shipping, may be unfamiliar with ship vetting. This includes ship's staff, managers, operational and commercial staff. This may be the case even when LNG shipping companies also operate oil, gas or chemical ships.

Similarly there are elements of the LNG trade which vetting departments, dealing largely with other marine trades need to appreciate.

2.3 Ship/Shore Compatibility

Ship/Shore compatibility studies for LNG ships calling at a terminal for the first time, are very detailed and will not normally be handled by vetting departments.

SIGTTO has produced a template of factors to be considered when carrying out a ship/shore compatibility assessment to facilitate this task for LNG operations. This template is freely available for download from the SIGTTO web site.

Ship shore compatibility studies are an assessment of the ability of the ship to fit the terminal, physically and operationally. Such studies involve examination of such items as those listed in Box 2.1.

Additionally an up to date HVPQ, and the following publications, can assist in the preparation and exchange of data for compatibility purposes.

- *Port Information Questionnaire for Liquefied Gas Terminals* [4]

- *Ship Information Questionnaire for Gas Carriers* [5]

General

- port name, ship name, general procedure to grant port approval

- shipping agents, utilities

Main characteristics

- port, ship

Confirmation between shore and ship

- fender/flat body (arrangement, strength)

- loading arms and manifold lay-outs (loading arm/manifold, arms envelopes)

- arms/cargo pumps/compressors (arms–loading, LN2, F.O., D.O., F.W. hose)

- mooring line/winch (QRH/winch number, strength, tail rope, lay-out, design weather criteria for mooring forces calculation

- gangway/support (position of gangway, gangway support, gangway working area, weight of gangway on support)

- service platform

- safety items (ESD, tension monitoring, approach meter, bonding cable, fire fighting)

- communications (communication link, telephone sets, ship/shore link not provided)

Procedures between shore and ship

- loading/unloading operations manual, post docking procedures, emergency procedures, port information book, contingency plan

Box 2.1 – Example of items which may be considered in a ship/shore compatibility study

2.4 Transparency

Where an LNG ship is engaged in a long-term project, the benefits of regular SIRE inspections may not be immediately apparent. The safety record of LNG ships is extremely good, with very few serious incidents. These results show that owners and operators of LNG ships have put considerable care and effort into crew training and ship maintenance, commensurate with equity, resulting in a high level of confidence. Additionally LNG ships have been managed by a relatively small number of operators who have had, in many cases, an equity interest in the projects.

In order that LNG Shipping can continue to maintain a high level of operational and safety awareness as the industry expands, the need for transparency becomes increasingly important. All stakeholders in the LNG transportation sector are expected to be open and transparent with their operations. By making all ship inspection reports available to Port State, Flag State and industry participants, the industry will be able to demonstrate commitment to safety and operational excellence.

To achieve a situation where all or most LNG ships are inspected regularly, will take some time. LNG operations are integrated across the value chain, requiring the co-operation and understanding of several parties, each of whom may represent substantial investment.

2.5 Flexibility and Availability

Regular SIRE inspections of LNG ships will increase trading flexibility. Many of the new short term charters are not single voyage, but are still for a much shorter period than traditionally used in LNG projects. Such cargoes can be the result of a project producing an excess quantity of gas, or when there is an increased demand, for example in winter. Many are the result of cargo swaps. Swaps can result in shorter voyages and thus significantly reduced costs and this practice is a growing facet of the LNG sector.

The sequence of activities leading up to the short term hire of an LNG ship is different from the established spot market activity of the oil trades. There is rarely more than one ship nominated for a given contract and the ship identity is usually known about a month in advance. All the elements of the cargo sale and purchase and the chartering contracts are negotiated in parallel, and then agreed simultaneously.

For a swap, the suppliers may still have to meet their obligation to provide gas to the receivers, so another vessel may also need to be vetted and hired.

Thus it is important for LNG ships to be acceptable to all of the parties concerned, and to be able to demonstrate that they are of an appropriate standard. Contracts often include clauses or subjects, giving the parties the right to vet and subsequently reject a nominated vessel if it falls below an acceptable standard. Such clauses include a notice period reasonable to both parties. i.e. giving sufficient time to nominate a replacement vessel, but not so far in advance as to invalidate any vetting decision.

Rejection of a vessel can have serious implications, for example new discharge ports may have to be found, with associated boil-off implications and the supplier is still contracted to supply the original quantity of gas. Another vessel will need to be found, which may well cause delays, due to the limited LNG tonnage available for short term hire.

Vessels which maintain a current SIRE report and whose managers and ship's staff are familiar with vetting will thus have improved flexibility. It should be noted, that any inspection report will need to be evaluated. Inspection alone does not mean that a ship will be accepted for use.

2.6 Inspections and Sire

In order to be able to demonstrate transparency and to facilitate flexibility, LNG shipping requires an appropriate inspection programme.

SIGTTO recommends that the SIRE inspection programme is used for the inspection of LNG ships.

This is because SIRE is an established, non-profit making and proven system, based on the marine expertise and experience of OCIMF members. The VIQ is a thoroughly researched and continuously improving document which provides a uniform structure and a factual reporting approach. The inspection process is appropriate for the LNG trade and SIRE involves an appropriate length of inspection, with an appropriate length and style of inspection report.

The inspector accreditation process is designed to ensure inspectors are appropriately qualified and experienced. There is a current shortage of gas accredited inspectors and SIRE provides a means through which this can be addressed.

The SIRE system is accessible by government bodies and third parties and provides a means for the industry to demonstrate that LNG shipping is safe.

It is a system with which many users are already familiar. It is not a check-list approach, but requires marine expertise to produce and to interpret. SIGTTO believes that this is an important factor in making accurate assessments of ship quality. This robust system is appropriate for the high level of investment involved in LNG shipping.

In common with many business activities, timely planning is essential for efficient and effective operations. The practicalities of carrying out inspections of LNG ships will require co-operation between vetting departments, inspectors, agents, ship managers, terminal staff and ship's staff. Communication in advance and a clear understanding of the inspection objectives and procedures by all parties, will ensure vessel access and inspection are not unnecessarily hindered.

2.7 Age

Age alone is not an indicator of ship quality. Age is a factor which may be taken into account in the vetting process.

At the time of writing, approximately 30% of the world's LNG fleet is over 20 years old. In general such vessels are operated by a small group of reputable operators and have been built and maintained to a high standard by a similarly select group of shipyards and are limited to a very small group of containment designers.

LNG ships are constructed in accordance with successive "Gas Carrier Codes", agreed by governments internationally under the auspices of the International Maritime Organisation (IMO). These codes recognise the potential hazards posed by liquefied gas cargoes and impose extensive and specific standards for their construction and subsequent operation. Cargo tanks are independent of ships' hull, being protectively located within ships' structures, above a double bottom and in board of the outer hull. As a result LNG ships have a greater structural integrity than that found in most other classes of ship and demonstrate an exceptional resistance to grounding and collision damage.

LNG ships are an integral part of the value chain in an LNG Project and as such the vessels benefit from increased initial investment in their design and construction. Because of the nature and criticality of the trade this involvement continues throughout the life of the vessel, commensurate with the needs of the project. The long term strategic horizon of these high capital projects also ensures the individual asset value in the LNG ship is maintained throughout and beyond its (and the projects) envisaged lifespan.

2.8 Clearances

As described in Section 1, a nominated vessel may be referred to a vetting department for a clearance. The factors described in Section 1 will be taken into account including inspection. If the vetting department has not inspected the vessel before, the internet enabled SIRE Enhanced Report Manager (webSERM) database will be checked, to see if a downloadable report exists. If a report does not exist the vetting department may need to inspect the vessel before the ship can be evaluated. This could take some time and could result in the business being delayed or ultimately not going ahead. It should also be noted, that clearance will be subject to the results of the inspection.

3 Specific Advice and Recommendations

This section contains SIGTTO advice and recommendations to the key stakeholders involved in LNG vetting, based on the explanations in Sections 1 and 2.

3.1 To Inspectors and Contracting Inspecting Companies

Inspectors and contracting inspecting companies inspecting LNG ships should:

- use the SIRE inspection programme for the inspection of LNG ships.

- follow the OCIMF guidelines on the conduct of a SIRE inspection. See Appendix 2.

- be familiar with the contents of the OCIMF/SIGTTO publication *Inspection Guidelines for Ships Carrying Liquefied Gases in Bulk.* [3]

- carry their OCIMF SIRE inspector's identification card, to an inspection.

- request agencies to notify terminals when there are changes to the inspection schedule.

- recognise that inspections may not be able to commence immediately on arrival due to customs, immigration or other operational priorities.

- be aware of the demands that an inspection puts on the ship's staff.

3.2 To Vetting Departments

Vetting departments should:

- be aware that LNG ships may need to be vetted well in advance of use due to the nature of the business.

- be aware that age alone is not an indicator of LNG ship quality.

- appoint SIRE gas accredited inspectors to inspect LNG ships.

- use the SIRE inspection programme for the inspection of LNG ships.

- consider the use of third party SIRE inspection reports in their vetting decisions.

3.3 To LNG Charterers, Brokers and Commercial Operators

Individuals engaged in the chartering of LNG ships on a short-term basis should:–

- recognise that a SIRE inspection may be required as part of normal business practice.

- facilitate such inspection, where possible through industry contacts and timely promulgation of explanatory information contained in this document.

- be aware that LNG ships may need to be vetted well in advance of use due to the nature of the business.

- recognise that transparency is in the best interest of LNG shipping. This can partly be achieved through a system of regular SIRE inspections of all LNG ships, which will also improve trading flexibility.

- recognise that vetting departments have a responsibility to operate a quality assurance evaluation process and have established procedures in place, which have a time element. Therefore, where possible, due notification of intended use should be given to vetting departments to allow the normal vetting processes to take place without delay to the business.

- recognise that time will be required to resolve ship compatibility issues for LNG ships calling at a terminal for the first time. Appropriate allowance should be made to facilitate this process.

- ensure that contracts contain appropriate clauses concerning ability to vet, inspect and reject a ship.

3.4 To LNG Ship Managers/Owners/ Pool Operators

Managers of LNG ships should:

- recognise that a SIRE inspection may be required as a routine part of the process of chartering an LNG ship.

- facilitate such inspections, where requested by charterers.

- explain the need for vetting to ship and office staff, by using this and other applicable material resources.

- familiarise vessel and office staff with the vetting process, and particularly with the inspection system and the VIQ, so that inspections and their follow-up proceed optimally.

- recognise that a current SIRE report will still require evaluation as a part of the clearance process.

- recognise that transparency is in the best interest of LNG shipping. This can partly be achieved through a system of regular SIRE inspections of all LNG ships, which will also improve their trading flexibility. Therefore managers are encouraged to arrange for regular SIRE inspections of each vessel under their control. Inspection frequency requirements of vetting departments may vary.

- avoid scheduling a ship inspection at the same time as other operations which place demands on ship's staff and/or could affect the safety of operations or the quality of the inspection. Consideration should be given to postponing inspections if other operations are to take place, such as Class or Flag surveys or large crew changes.

- recognise that the inspector, in his capacity as a SIRE inspector, is not authorised to give any indication of ship acceptability or non-acceptability (See Appendix 2) and cannot make a decision or a recommendation, regarding the use of the vessel.

- ensure that vessels are given adequate notice of an impending inspection and are informed of the objectives so that preparations can be made.

- following an inspection, respond promptly (within two weeks) to the inspecting company and to SIRE, with any comments on the observations made. Managers responding to reports should be familiar with the OCIMF VIQ [1], in particular the section regarding Conduct of Inspections (Appendix 2). For reasons of completeness, even if the inspection report does not contain any adverse comment or observation, the ship operator should submit a comment to SIRE that acknowledges that fact.

- maintain an up to date HVPQ in SIRE. The Intertanko booklet [2] includes some guidelines on the completion of the HVPQ.

3.5 To Ship's Staff

Ship's staff employed on LNG ships should:

- familiarise themselves with the vetting process. In particular the OCIMF VIQ [1] guidance regarding the preparation and conduct of inspections should be consulted (See Appendix 2).

- make appropriate preparations for inspections. Some guidance on preparation for an inspection is given in the Intertanko booklet [2]. Commercial publications and videos are also available. The preparation of documentation, including a current HVPQ and officer's qualifications matrix can save considerable time.

- anticipate the demands on the human resources available, having due regard to the requirements of the STCW Code [9] and other applicable requirements in respect of work/rest hours. The work/rest hours of staff most likely to be involved in the inspection and concurrent operations, should be considered in advance.

3.6 To LNG Terminal Operators

LNG Terminal operators should:

- ensure that appropriate personnel are familiar with the need for inspectors to access vessels, and ensure such access is not unnecessarily hindered.

- where appropriate subscribe to the SIRE programme.

- utilise the SIRE Programme Reports to assist with the evaluation of quality and ensure that appropriate marine expertise is available for interpretation of SIRE reports.

- where appropriate, liaise with agents for information regarding the scheduling of appointed inspectors and terminal security procedures, to ensure access is not unnecessarily hindered.

- if providing feedback on vessels to their principals, discuss any observations with ship's staff on site at the time.

- endeavour to make terminal particulars information readily available, e.g. via a port web site.

- consider inspector access and egress when developing or modifying Port Facility Security Plans in line with the ISPS Code [10].

3.7 To Ship's Agents

Ship's agents should:

- ensure that terminals and ships are advised as soon as possible of an inspector's intended schedule and of any changes that may have been made.

- advise inspectors of any terminal requirements for entry, such as identification required.

- advise inspectors of any changes in the vessel's berthing schedule.

References – Documents Referenced in the Text

1.   *SIRE VIQ, 2nd Edition 2000. OCIMF*

2.   *A Guide to the Vetting Process, 5th Edition 2003. Intertanko*

3.   *Inspection Guidelines for Ships Carrying Liquefied Gases in Bulk, 2nd Edition 1998. OCIMF/SIGTTO*

4.   *Port Information Questionnaire for Liquefied Gas Terminals, 1st Edition 1998. SIGTTO*

5.   *Ship Information Questionnaire for Gas Carriers, 2nd Edition 1998. OCIMF, SIGTTO*

6.   *The International Safety Guide for Oil Tankers and Terminals, (ISGOTT), 4th Edition. OCIMF, ICS, IAPH*

7.   *Liquefied Gas Handling Principles, 3rd Edition, 2000. SIGTTO*

8.   *The Tanker Safety Guide (Liquefied Gas), 1996. (ICS)*

9.   *Seafarers Training Certification and Watchkeeping Code (STCW Code), 1995. IMO*

10. *International Ship and Port Facility Security Code (ISPS Code), 2002. IMO*

11. *Safety of Life at Sea Convention (SOLAS), 1974. IMO*

12. *International Management Code for the Safe Operation of Ships and for Pollution Prevention – the International Safety Management (ISM) Code, 1997. IMO*

Bibliography – documents other than those referenced, providing related subject matter

1. A Glossary of LNG Terms. Exxon Mobil Gas Marketing

2. INCOTERMS 2000. International Chamber of Commerce

3. Keeping up Standards – Ship Vetting Inspections for Bulk Oil Carriers (22 Mins) - Videotel Code No.- 547 – Videotel

Items listed in this Bibliography are included for information only. SIGTTO does not necessarily endorse any of these documents nor any company or organisation listed.

Extract from the Ship Inspection Report (SIRE) Programme, Second Edition 2000 – OCIMF – Section I

Purpose and Scope

Original SIRE Programme

In 1993, OCIMF established a Ship Inspection Report (SIRE) Programme ("Original Programme") which enabled OCIMF Members to submit their ship inspection reports ("Reports" or "Report") to OCIMF for OCIMF's distribution to OCIMF Members and certain qualifying non-OCIMF Members. Such OCIMF Members and qualifying non-OCIMF Members are herein called "Programme Recipients".

Participation in the Original Programme, as either an inspecting OCIMF Member or a Programme Recipient, was strictly voluntary and each Programme Recipient determined independently how to evaluate the information contained in the Reports received from OCIMF.

Under the Original Programme, the operator ("Operator") of the ship which was the subject of a Report was given a copy of the Report and the opportunity to give written comment on the Report to both the inspecting OCIMF Member and to OCIMF.

An automated central computer System ("SIRE System") was set up in OCIMF's London offices to receive, store and distribute the Reports and any Operator comments. This System also created and fed a computerised Index giving pertinent information about the Reports and any ship Operator comments.

OCIMF Members inputted their Reports into the SIRE System by computer. These Reports were then electronically stored in this System. Paper copies of the Reports were also sent by the submitting OCIMF Members to the Operators via facsimile, mail or courier. Any Operator comments on the Reports were sent (via facsimile) by the Operator to the OCIMF Members submitting the Reports and to OCIMF's London offices. Upon receipt at OCIMF's offices, Operator comments were converted to, and stored in, electronic form in the SIRE System.

The above submission of Reports and Operator comments to OCIMF had to be made through the use of separate Cover Sheets. These Cover Sheets, which gave key details of the ship inspection covered by the Reports, were also stored in electronic form in the SIRE System.

By electronically scanning these separate Cover Sheets, the SIRE System automatically matched any Operator comment received with the appropriate Report, with the result that requesting Programme Recipients would receive both the Report and the Operator comment.

The SIRE System Index was accessed by computer or dumb terminal and allowed a Programme Recipient to view, download or print the Index. When ordered by Programme Recipients, Reports and any matching Operator comments in the SIRE System were converted from electronic form to paper and were automatically transmitted by facsimile to the Programme Recipients' pre-registered facsimile numbers.

Revised SIRE Programme

The Original Programme was revised in 1997. With the exception of the newly introduced ability of Programme Recipients to receive Reports and any Operator comments in electronic, as well as paper form, all the above described features of the Original Programme remained unchanged in the SIRE Programme.

Two major changes were, however, introduced in the Revised Programme. These two changes were:

1. A Uniform Vessel Inspection Procedure; and,

2. A Vessel Particular Questionnaire (VPQ)[1]

The SIRE Programme was again revised in 2000. This latest revision expands the current features of the above Inspection Procedure while also adding new components thereto and eliminates any option to receive Programme output in paper form.

The Outline which follows incorporates the above 1997 and 2000 revisions to the SIRE Programme.

1. Uniform Vessel Inspection Procedure

This Procedure has two elements i.e., *an Inspection Element* and a *Report Element.*

Inspection Element

The Inspection Element has three sub-elements as follows:

---

[1] Under the Original Programme, the inspecting OCIMF Member was free to choose whatever inspection protocol and report format it desired. The Uniform Vessel Inspection Procedure changed this. The Vessel Particular Questionnaire was a newly developed OCIMF document and was not part of the Original Programme.

Vessel Inspection Questionnaire. – This is the heart of the Inspection Element and thus, a document which the ship Inspector **must** use in the conduct of the ship inspection.[2] The Vessel Inspection Questionnaire ("VIQ") has a series of about 196 Key Questions separately and sequentially numbered relating to safety and pollution prevention, which, in most cases, are accompanied by guidance notes, sub-questions and source materials to aid the Inspector's response. The Key Questions are logically grouped into separate Chapters, with each Chapter focusing on a specific and separate area of ship safety and pollution prevention. While some of these Questions ask for informational response, such as ship size, particulars and dates, most of the Key Questions call for either a direct Yes, No, Not Seen or Not Applicable response. Except as noted in Section II hereof, the Inspector **must** answer all Key Questions. In certain circumstances, the Inspector is required to supplement his or her answers to Key Questions with explanatory comment. A space for Inspector comments is provided at the end of each Key Question and at the end of each VIQ Chapter.[3] This aspect is outlined in the next paragraph.

Where a Key Question is answered Yes, Inspector comment is, in most cases, not required. On the other hand, where a Key Question is answered No, the Inspector **must** specify and explain the nature of the non-compliance. Additionally, where a Key Question is answered with a Not Seen or Not Applicable, the Inspector **must** give the reason for the response. Finally, the Inspector is free to give comment at the end of a Key Question no matter how the Question is answered and/or at the end of any VIQ Chapter.

The Vessel Inspection Questionnaire document **must** be converted into, and answered in, electronic form. To accomplish the foregoing conversion and response, the Inspector must use a computer in conjunction with specialised OCIMF software.[4] Further, such VIQ response must, in turn, be electronically submitted to the SIRE System in order to create therein, a Report for distribution to Programme Recipients.

Inspector Manual (ROVIQ) – This Document is a new feature added by the 2000 SIRE Revisions. In short, the Manual is a reorganisation of the revised VIQ Key Questions, sub-questions and guidance notes to follow the order of the route that would normally be taken by an Inspector in the course of an inspection.[5] The Introductory portion of this Manual contains the same Mandatory and Permissive Inspection criteria set forth in Section III of this Document and *expands the Inspection Suggestions also found in the just mentioned Section*. The ROVIQ will be supplied by OCIMF only to Inspectors.[6]

Minimum Inspector Qualifications – This is another new feature introduced by the 2000 SIRE Revisions. This Item covers Inspector Qualifications, Mandatory Application of such Qualifications and Qualifications Administration as follows:

1. Inspector Qualifications

Certification

Inspectors must hold, or have held:

1. a Master's licence from a recognised flag State for vessels of 3,000 grt or more or

2. certification as Chief Engineer Officer for vessels powered by main propulsion of 3,000kw or more.

Work Experience

Inspectors:

1. must have at least five (5) years service aboard tankers, of which not less than two (2) years must have been as senior officer on board the type of vessel to be inspected and

2. shall hold or have held either a Dangerous Cargo Endorsement appropriate to the type of vessel to be inspected or proof of satisfactory training under the STCW Convention.

---

[2] The Revised Programme covers the inspection of bulk oil/product tankers (including combination carriers), bulk chemical tankers and gas carriers *only.*

[3] Insofar as the VIQ is concerned, the 2000 SIRE Revision consisted of an extensive rewording of existing Key Questions, sub-questions, guidance notes, the addition of some 21 new Key Questions and 62 sub-questions, together with new guidance notes. This amended – 2000-2nd Edition – is the version of the VIQ *which must now be used in the Revised Programme.*

[4] For the most efficient functioning of the Vessel Inspection Procedure, the Inspector should bring, or have available, a computer with the above required special OCIMF software. If these are not on board, the Inspector would have to make hand written responses to the Vessel Inspection Questionnaire document for computer entry after the inspection has been completed. If no computer is available, the Inspector must send such responses to either the Inspecting Company or the OCIMF Inspecting Member. The latter would then have to enter the paper response to the Questionnaire in an office computer using the special OCIMF software in order to produce the required electronic format.

[5] The ROVIQ is laid out on the assumption that an inspection takes the following course: a review of the vessel's Documentation, followed by inspection of the Wheelhouse and Navigation, followed by inspection of Communications, General External areas, Mooring, Main Deck, Pumproom, Cargo Control Room, the Engine Room, Steering Gear Room and finally, the Internal Accommodation. Supplementary Sections are included for the inspection of Chemical Tankers, Gas Carriers and Combination Carriers as may be applicable to the type of vessel being inspected.

[6] Each Inspector will receive from OCIMF (i) one full size copy of the ROVIQ (ii) one pocket size copy of the ROVIQ and (iii) one set of computer software containing the VIQ/ROVIQ Inspection Programme.

Knowledge

Inspectors must be able to demonstrate familiarity with, and knowledge of, International Regulations, Codes and Conventions and Industry Guidelines, Procedures and Standards appropriate to the type of vessels being inspected. Those should include, but not be limited to;

o Policies and Procedures required by ISM

o IMO Safety of Life at Sea Convention (SOLAS 74)

o IMO International Convention for the Prevention of Pollution from Ships (MARPOL 73/78)

o IMO International Regulations for the Preventing Sea Collisions at Sea (COLREGS)

o IMO Code for the Construction and Equipment of Ships Carrying Dangerous Chemicals in Bulk (IBC Code)

o IMO Code for the Construction and Equipment of Ships Carrying Dangerous Chemicals in Bulk (BCH Code)

o IMO Code for the Construction and Equipment of Ships Carrying Liquefied Gases in Bulk (IGC Code)

o IMO International Convention of Standards of training, Certification and Watchkeeping for Seafarers, 1978 as amended in 1995 (STCW Convention)

o ICS Tanker Safety Guide (Chemicals)

o ICS Tanker Safety Guide (Liquefied Gas)

o ICS Guide to Helicopter/Ship Operations

o OCIMF/ICS/IAPH International Safety Guide for Oil Tankers and Terminals (ISGOTT)

o OCIMF/ICS Clean Seas Guide for Tankers

o OCIMF/ICS Prevention of Oil Spillages Through Cargo Pumproom Sea Valves

o OCIMF/ICS Ship to Ship Transfer Guide (Petroleum)

o OCIMF Recommendation for Oil Tanker Manifolds and Associated Equipment

o OCIMF Mooring Equipment Guidelines

o OCIMF Effective Mooring

o USCG Regulations for Tankers (USCG 33 CFR 155-156) (If applicable)

o OCIMF Guidelines for the Control of Drugs and Alcohol abroad Ship (1995)

Capabilities

Inspectors must:

- be physically capable of conducting a full and complete inspection according to the requirements of the VIQ and

- be capable of communicating proficiently in written and spoken English.

2. Mandatory Application

The above Qualifications only apply to Inspectors performing their first SIRE commissioned inspection subsequent to the Effective Date of the 2000 revisions.

3. Qualifications Administration

OCIMF will not administer an Inspecting Member's compliance with the above Qualifications but will leave this up to the Member's self administration.[7]

Report Element

This is the Report reflecting the ship inspection results. The Report does not replicate the pages of the VIQ document. Rather, it consists of a further electronic conversion of the Inspector's electronic VIQ responses/comments into an abbreviated and reformatted uniform Report form which is producible in both a paper and electronic version. This transformation is made possible through the use of a computer and the same specialised OCIMF software, mentioned above. The conversion of the VIQ response into a paper Report can be done either by the OCIMF Member or by the SIRE System. The conversion of the VIQ response into an electronic Report to be stored in the SIRE System for Programme distribution can only be accomplished in the System. This conversion takes place when the electronic VIQ response enters the System.

The Inspector must transmit the electronically completed VIQ to the OCIMF Member ordering the Inspection. The OCIMF Member will then be able to computer view or print out a paper version of the Report.

In order to submit the Report to SIRE, the Member must transmit the electronically completed VIQ to the SIRE System. Upon receipt in the SIRE System, the System will, as noted above, automatically convert the completed

---

[7] OCIMF is considering establishing an Inspector Accreditation Requirement for all Inspectors.

VIQ into an electronic Report in the required uniform format and then electronically store same in the System. Using a computer and the above specialised OCIMF software, the Member must also produce a paper version of the Report and send same via mail, courier or fax to the Operator.

The Operator has the opportunity to pass written comment on the Report via facsimile to the inspecting OCIMF Member and to the SIRE System. Upon receipt in the SIRE System, the Operator comment will be converted into electronic form and then be electronically stored in the System.

By reason of the change effected by the 2000 SIRE Revisions, Programme Recipients will no longer have the option to receive the Report (and any Operator comment) either electronically or in paper form. The latter documents are now only available electronically.[8]

The above discussed specialised OCIMF software is combined into a single software package. OCIMF will supply this package free of charge to OCIMF Members. OCIMF will not supply a computer.

As the Report will be a truncated and reformatted version of the Inspector responses to the Vessel Inspection Questionnaire Document (2nd Edition – 2000), the Operator will have to have in its possession a (blank) paper copy of the full Questionnaire Document to be able to understand the Report. The Inspecting OCIMF Member is required to ensure that the ship Operator has in its possession a (blank) paper copy of this Document no later than the date the Member sends the Report to the Operator. Like the Operator, a Programme Recipient must also be in possession of a (blank) paper copy of this Document to decipher the Report. OCIMF will ensure that all Programme Recipients timely receive the Document.

2. Vessel Particulars Questionnaire (VPQ)

OCIMF has published a Vessel Particulars Questionnaire (VPQ) which asks over 700 separate questions about ship particulars and required or customary on board documents which are of a permanent or semi-permanent nature, primarily related to safety and pollution prevention. The questions are sequentially numbered and are logically grouped into separate Chapters. This document is separate and apart from the Vessel Inspection Questionnaire.

The VPQ has been incorporated as an *optional* element under the Revised Programme. When used in conjunction with the Revised Programme, the VPQ is to be answered by the Operator, with a separate VPQ for each operated ship and then sent to the SIRE System.

Like the VIQ, the response to the VPQ must be in electronic form to be accepted into the SIRE System. This will require the Operator to answer the document by utilising a computer in conjunction with specialised OCIMF software. This software will also allow a paper printout of the VPQ response. The software will be provided (free of charge) by OCIMF to Operators. As with the VIQ, no computer will be provided by OCIMF.

To best complement an inspection under the Revised Programme, a completed and up to date VPQ (in either electronic or paper form) should be on board at the time of a ship inspection and have been sent to the SIRE System for inclusion in the Revised Programme. *SIRE, however, will accept a VPQ for a ship only if there is a Report for that ship in the SIRE System. The Report can be one submitted under the Original Programme or the Revised Programme.*

The SIRE System Index will indicate the VPQ responses received. These responses will be available (in electronic form only) to any Programme Recipient.

Once a VPQ response is received into the SIRE System, there should be no need for an Operator to make any further VPQ transmissions to SIRE except to correct or keep current, previously submitted VPQ information.

When used, as above described in connection with the Revised Programme, the VPQ has two main functions;

(1) to assist the ship Inspector by having at hand completed and up to date basic ship information which the Inspector may need during the inspection – thus allowing the Inspector to better utilise inspection time on board and

(2) to assist the OCIMF inspecting Member and Programme Recipients in their individual and separate overall evaluations of the ship.

---

[8] OCIMF is considering adding to the SIRE System, an option which will allow Inspecting Members to electronically transmit Reports to Operators (instead of only paper Reports as now) and/or for Operators to transmit Operator comments to the Inspecting Members and the SIRE System also electronically (instead of only paper comments as now). If the foregoing option is added to the SIRE System, it will be announced in a SIRE Circular distributed to OCIMF Members and, through them, to Operators.

Conduct of Inspections

Mandatory Inspection Requirements

The following are mandatory requirements which ship Inspectors **must** follow in the conduct of their shipboard inspection in order for their Reports to meet the requirements of the Revised Programme:

Inspectors:

1. **must** tick one box for each Key Question;

2. **must,** where there are sub-question(s) and/or Guidance to a Key Question, consider all the sub-question(s) and Guidance to determine how the Key Question should be answered;

3. **must** answer every Key Question and consider every sub-question as written;

4. **must** use objective evidence when answering each Key Question (The assurance of the vessel's staff is insufficient evidence or proof);

5. **must** include a comment in the box under a Key Question when it is answered **'No', 'Not Seen'** or **'Not Applicable'** and/or where the VIQ requires comment no matter how a Key Question is answered;

6. **must not** use a 'Yes' response to any Question where an Inspector's observation or comment contains negative elements (If there is such negative observation or comment then the answer to that Question should be 'No');

7. **must not,** in any Comment or Additional Comments, include -

   i. any overall or partial ship rating or indication of ship acceptability non-acceptability;

   ii. any matter unrelated to the topic of a VIQ Chapter and, in particular, any matter unrelated to ship safety and pollution prevention; and,

   iii. any overall, Chapter ending or other partial summary of the Inspector's findings;

8. **must** give the factual basis and specific reasons for any opinions or subjective comments made by the Inspector;

9. **must** note any deficiencies or Inspector observed conditions as to which action was taken whilst the Inspector was on board and

10. **must** not offer any comments or opinions with regard to actions to be taken in respect of any deficiencies or observed conditions noted by the Inspector.

Permissive Inspection Actions

Inspectors **may:**

1. include comments on any Key Question, even where the Key Question is answered with a **'Yes'**;

2. respond to Key Questions or provide comments on the basis of material not included in the Guidance specified for the Key Question but must note this reliance and explain reason for the reliance;

3. include in the **'Additional Comments'** for each Chapter, any comments in respect of the subject matter covered by the Chapter additional to those that the Inspector may make in response to the specific Key Questions in the Chapter and

4. ignore sub-questions which may not be applicable to either the vessel or the vessel's cargo.

Inspection Suggestions

1. The Inspector should introduce himself or herself to the Master or the Master's authorised deputy, explain the scope of the inspection and discuss the order in which it will be carried out. The Master should be invited to accompany the Inspector on the inspection or to appoint one of the vessel's officers.

2. Unless authorised by the OCIMF Inspecting Member, inspections should not take place at night.

3. The Inspector should set a good example with respect to his or her own personal safety procedures whilst on board the vessel and in the terminal and should wear appropriate personal protection equipment at all times.

4. Electrical or electronic equipment of non-approved type, whether mains or battery powered, should not be active, switched on or used within gas-hazardous areas. This includes torches, radios, mobile telephones, radio pagers, calculators, computers, photographic equipment and any other portable equipment that is electrically powered but not

approved for operation in a gas-hazardous area. It should be borne in mind that equipment such as mobile telephones and radio pagers, if switched on, can be activated remotely and a hazard can be generated by the alerting or calling mechanism and, in the case of telephones, by the natural response to answer the call.

5. The Inspector should consider requesting that equipment be run and tested to confirm that it is in operational order and that officers and crew are familiar with its operation, but should ensure that such requests do not cause delay or interfere with the safety and normal operation of the vessel.

6. **It should be recognised that the overall objective of the inspection is to provide the user of a SIRE Report with a factual record of the vessel's condition and standard of operation at the time of the inspection and, in turn, allow an assessment of the risk that use of the vessel might pose.**

7. **It is important that any observations that the Inspector intends to record in the VIQ are pointed out and discussed 'on site' at the time.** This ensures that the crew fully understand the nature of the observations and it can also save discussion at the end of the inspection. Sheets are included with the Inspector Manual (ROVIQ) for the recording of observations noted during the inspection.

8. Tank entry should only be undertaken if a suitable safe opportunity exists, it is approved by the Inspecting Member and port regulations allow. At all times the most stringent safety procedures should be followed and an entry permit should be issued by an appropriate ship's officer. The tests and precautions contained in ISGOTT Chapter 11 should be observed and an entry into an enclosed space should not be made without the full knowledge and consent of the master.

Extract from "A Guide to The Vetting Inspections", 5th Edition 2003, Intertanko

Remember that the inspection result establishes whether the tanker is operated in a safe way in accordance with valid rules and regulations.

The onboard inspection can only be successful **if the tanker is prepared** for the inspection. The inspector who is to carry out the inspection will start to collect impressions from even before the time he takes his first step onto the gangway and will continue to do so until he takes the last step off the gangway when leaving the tanker after completing the inspection.

Almost all inspectors are former seafarers who from both deck and engine room experience are able to assess a tanker. Most likely the first impression formed from the time the tanker is sighted until the inspector's arrival at the Master's cabin will be the strongest. It will be subjective at this point. Inspectors will undertake the inspection of the tanker looking for objective criteria by which to judge the tanker. It is a fact of life that, however subconscious the urge may be, the inspector will look for objective evidence to support his initial subjective opinion. Thus the importance of the route from ship to side to Master's cabin should not be underestimated. Remember you do not get a second chance to make a first impression.

Preparation for the Inspection

Make sure that the inspection is scheduled at a convenient time for the vessel, so it does not conflict with other inspections or similar matters. This could easily be arranged through the port agent.

Make sure that each head of department has completed his own inspection before arrival at the port and that any deficiencies have been reported/corrected. This should be incorporated into the normal routine guidelines.

An effective way of administering this is to introduce a Self-Assessment form covering the following areas. The allocation of tasks for the specific areas is a suggestion and will depend on individual, company defined areas of responsibility.

- Tanker Particulars
  Master
- Certification/Documentation
  Master
- Crew Management
  Master
- Safety Management
  Master/Chief Engineer
- Lifesaving Equipment
  Second/Third Mate
- Fire Fighting Equipment
  Chief Engineer
- Pollution Prevention
  Chief Officer
- Cargo/Ballast System
  Chief Officer
- Inert Gas System
  First Engineer
- COW Installation
  Chief Officer
- Mooring Equipment
  Chief Officer
- Bridge Equipment
  Second Officer
- Radio Equipment
  Radio Officer/Master
- Engine Room and Steering
  Chief Engineer
- Load Lines Items
  Chief Officer
- Chemical Supplement
  Chief Officer

This is meant as an example. The next layer in this table is the delegation given to petty officers and in turn, to the rest of the crew. It is important to have a working organisation that delegates. This will achieve an understanding all the way down through the ranks.

Prior to the inspection preparations can be made in certain areas.

The Inspector may need to have a copy of the following:

- Classification Document
- Certificate of Registry
- Cargo Ship Safety Construction Certificate
- Cargo Ship Safety Equipment Certificate
- Safety Radiotelegraphy Certificate
- Load Line Certificate
- IMO Certificate of Fitness
- IOPP Certificate & Supplement
- Certificate of Financial Responsibility
- A Crew List

- A Drawing of the vessel's cargo tank arrangement
- Vessel's Safe Manning Document.

The following should be available for Inspection
(some are not applicable to all vessels); Masters should lay out the certificates in the same order as they appear in the VPQ/VIQ. This saves time and creates a good impression of ordered preparation.

- Officers' Licenses
- Health Certificates
- P&A Manual
- Approved COW Manual
- Approved Ballast Manual
- Oil/Cargo record book
- Oil transfer procedures
- Garbage log for compliance with MARPOL Annex V
- Proof of cargo hose/piping testing
- Proof of fixed and portable fire fighting equipment servicing
- Proof of professional servicing of breathing apparatus
- Proof of life raft servicing
- Settings for vessel's PV valves
- Shipping document and cargo manifest
- Certificate of inhabitation or stabilisation of cargo
- Declaration of Inspection if transferring bunkers
- Cargo Information Cards for the cargo on board
- Inert Gas Manual
- Waiver Letters, if any
- Vessel Response Plan
- Safety Manual
- Vessel Operation Manual
- Company's policy for upgrading and training.

Be prepared to calibrate and/or demonstrate the proper operation of:

- Combustible gas detectors or fixed gas detection system
- Oxygen analyser
- Toxic gas detector
- Overboard discharge monitor
- Cargo pump Emergency shutdown and bearing alarms
- High level alarms
- Overfill alarms
- Quick closing valves.

Be prepared to demonstrate the proper operation of the following systems/alarms:

- Inert Gas systems alarms
- Oily water separator
- Fire fighting systems
- Steering gear
- Emergency generator
- Engine room ventilation shutdowns
- Fuel oil cut-off valves

In addition, the following items may be checked and should be ready:

- Firemen's outfits
- International shore connection
- Navigation equipment
- Charts, publications, and corrections
- EPIRB, pyrotechnics and hydrostatic releases
- Flame screens, bunker tanks
- Suitable paint locker
- Marine sanitation device

Reference should also be made to the particular requirements of the oil major inspecting the vessel.

The following items are of vital importance as these provide an overall impression of the vessel, and will play an essential part in how the inspection will be conducted.

1. **Gangway:** Correctly arranged – is the gangway net rigged? Is there a life ring nearby?

2. **Signs:** All warning signs posted[1]

3. **Crew:** All crew working on deck should have hard hats and the necessary protection gear.

4. **Deck Watch:** Is he present in the area? Hard-hat emergency equipment[2] handy, necessary for cargo loading/discharging; walkie-talkie; ask the inspector who he is and who he wants to see; confirm with Duty Officer that this is OK. One crew member should follow the inspector to the ship office.

5. **Fire Equipment at the Manifold:** Correctly rigged and present.

6. **Deck:** Clean, free of oil/water and obstructions.

7. **Scuppers:** Blocked, emergency pump in position and discharge connected.

8. **Cargo Information:** Make sure that all personnel involved in the cargo operation are briefed regarding what cargoes are being loaded/discharged, particularly the deck watch. All MSDS[3] to be up and easily readable.

9. **Emergency Equipment:** Working, present and clearly marked.

10. **Moorings:** In good order, no lines on the winch ends.

11. **Accommodation:** All doors closed, clean and in proper order.

---

[1] No visitors, Hazardous cargo
[2] As per emergency instructions. This could refer to safety goggles, rubber boots, rubber gloves.
[3] Material Safety Data Sheets

APPENDIX 3

The Inspection

Make sure that the inspector is accompanied on the vessel during the inspection. The best people to do this would be the Master, Chief Engineer, Chief Officer and the First Assistant Engineer (Second Engineer), who can divide the areas of inspection amongst themselves.

Normally, the inspector will start by checking all certificates[4] and documentation with the Master. He will then move into the areas listed opposite. However, it must be remembered that the order and schedule of the inspection can be changed to achieve less disturbance to the normal operations onboard. The inspector will have a pre-planned inspection format, which he will wish to follow, though there is nothing to stop different sections being done in a different order. With the new OCIMF VPQ, much of the data referring to the tanker will have been completed in advance. Make sure that you have a completed up-to-date copy available for the inspector as this will save much time.

Below are the most common deficiencies found in all areas:

1. Bridge and Radio Room
2. Cargo Control Room and Tank Deck
3. Engine Room and Steering Gear
4. Accommodation/Galley

Bridge and Radio Room

The most common deficiencies encountered in the Bridge/Radio room areas are related to publications.

- Passage plan only pilot to pilot. Ensure that the filed passage plan covers berth to berth navigation
- Missing publications or old editions onboard when new publications have been issued
- Missing Master's standing orders and night order book
- No logs for gyro error
- No entry of position on the navigation chart during transit of pilotage to berth
- Chart corrections not logged correctly

Cargo Control Room and Tank Deck

- No cargo/ballast plan available
- Hydraulic leaks on deck
- Officers and ratings not wearing hard hats on deck
- No screens inside the vents for the ballast tanks
- No calibration gas for gas detection instruments
- Crew not wearing personal protection gear
- No policy for entering tanks

Engine Room and Steering Gear

- No procedures or instructions posted for foam system
- Emergency steering procedures not posted properly in steering gear room
- Hot work procedures not used or not present in the manuals
- No safety guidelines available for engine room/ workshop welding equipment
- No eye protection warning notices posted for engine workshop machinery
- No clean goggles by grinders and lathes

Accommodation/Galley

- Untidy
- Overhead ventilation greasy – fire hazard
- Accommodation ventilators with no identification labels

After the Inspection

All inspectors should sit down and discuss observations and comments after the inspection is completed. If not, the Master should record a written objection that this has not taken place and inform his company immediately.

The inspector gives the Master a written list of the observations found.

- Correct all observations as soon as possible
- Send the report to the head office or department in charge
- Complete the Inspector Feedback Form and send it together with the report (a copy is to be found at the back of this booklet).

The Master must demand a copy of these findings in writing so that should there be a change between what is said in the Master's cabin and what appears in the report, this can be taken up later by the company ashore.

When the Inspector is discussing with the Master the issues that he has found, it is quite often possible that there has been a misunderstanding or that the Inspector has become confused with another ship that he has recently done. At this point in time, it is relatively easy for such an error to be cleared up and the Master should take every step to achieve this. In addition, the Master should not feel intimidated by the Inspector. This is of course easier said than done, particularly if the Master feels that he has less English skills than the Inspector in front of him. It is unlikely that the Master will be able to get the Inspector to delete a finding or an observation, even if it has been fixed, (though this should be included in the report). On the other hand, he should be able to get additional comments added which mitigate the finding or explain why it is the case.

---

[4] Make sure that copies are available if the agent has taken certificates ashore.

As an example, the Inspector may find that there is a large bubble in the magnetic compass. The Master, (if it is the case), should point out to the Inspector that he already aware of this, that he has already ordered a new compass, that he has the requisition number and it is due to be delivered in the Port later on today, or whatever is the example that you choose to use. Certainly this would then turn an observation into an utterly reasonable state of affairs from one that might be considered rather more serious if it was not followed up properly by the Master.

ISPS Code

There is little doubt that vettings conducted after 1 July 2004 will be expanded to audit that the vessel carries a valid International Ship Security Certificate (ISSC) and that it operated in conformity with its Ship Security Plan. This will be taken as evidence that the Ship Security Officer (SSO) has received the required training and that the seafarers hold the necessary level of security awareness. There is no international requirement for SSOs to undergo formal training prior to 1 July 2004 but individual flag states may decide differently.

Classification societies are currently in the process of acquiring their status as Responsible Security Organizations (RSOs) and are educating their inspectors for these new work requirements.

Owners will, in the time leading up to the above deadline, be well advised to make preparations ensuring that the best possible internal or external training is provided and that proof of attendance is kept onboard to prove conformity. It is noteworthy that IMO (MSC77) decided that even minor non-conformities in compliance with the ISPS Code requirements may lead to suspension of the ISSC.

INTERTANKO is a member of the IMO Validation Panel in order to take active part in establishing Model Courses for the training of the SSO, the Company Security Officer (CSO) and the Port Security Officer (PFSO). These model courses are expected to be ready in September 2003.

Related Web Sites

SIGTTO	http://www.sigtto.org/
OCIMF	http://www.ocimf.com/
CDI	http://www.cdi.org.uk/main.html
Equasis	http://www.equasis.org/
Paris MOU	http://www.parismou.org/
Tokyo MOU	http://www.tokyo-mou.org/
USCG PSIX	http://psix.uscg.mil/psix2/
AMSA	http://www.amsa.gov.au/
Intertanko	http://www.intertanko.com
Videotel	http://www.videotel.com/
IMO	http://www.imo.org
IACS	http://www.iacs.org.uk/index1.htm
Witherbys	http://www.witherbys.com

The following table provides a summary of common terminology used in ship vetting, with a brief definition for each. This table serves to clarify the intended meaning of terminology used in this document.

Term	Description
Assessor	An individual employed within a vetting department, to make vetting decisions.
CAP	Condition Assessment Programme. CAP is a verification of the actual condition of the vessel, based upon detailed inspection and function testing, thickness measurements and strength calculations, carried out by the Classification Society. It is a programme requested by a ship owner, and should not be confused with CAS (Condition Assessment Scheme) which is a statutory requirement for certain vessels under MARPOL.
Casualty Data (Incident Records)	Records of a vessel's casualty history are often maintained by vetting departments. This is one of the elements used in assessing marine risk.
CDI	Chemical Distribution Institute (CDI) is an independent, non profit making organisation created to provide risk assessment systems for bulk liquids shipping and storage of liquids in bulk in 3rd party terminals for its participating chemical companies. It is a chemical industry ship inspection process and database, managed through joint representation by charterers and ship managers.
CDI Report	A report produced following an inspection by a CDI inspector using the CDI inspection format.
Classification Society	A classification society's work involves the development and implementation of published Rules and/or Regulations which will provide for the structural strength and watertight integrity of all essential parts of the hull and its appendages, and the safety and reliability of the propulsion and steering systems, and those other features and auxiliary systems which have been built into the ship in order to establish and maintain basic conditions on board.
Clearance (Screening)	The process of evaluating the risks associated with a proposed business venture involving a third party vessel. Where this system is used the freight trader or similar party will request a clearance for a vessel to be used for a specified voyage.
COA (Contract of Affreightment)	A cargo transportation arrangement whereby the owner agrees to transportation of a specified quantity of cargo over a set period of time in a vessel or series of vessels for the charterer. It consists of the base terms of agreement, (e.g. cargo quantity to be transported, period of agreement, cargo and ship nomination, scheduling, etc.) to which a governing pro forma voyage charter party is attached.
Commercial Operator	The department of an organisation responsible for arranging charters for its owned or bareboat chartered vessels, or any other company contracted to carry out such activity on their behalf.
Contracting Inspecting Companies	A company, which employs SIRE accredited inspectors, who may carry out inspections on behalf of an "Inspecting Company".
Evaluation (Rating)	An evaluation may be made following the review of information such as a SIRE report, which reflects the condition of the vessel at the time of the inspection.

Term	Description
Freight Trader	Individual employed in a commercial position to negotiate and arrange for the hire of ships. Freight traders are often the focal point for communications with the vetting department.
Fleet Profile	The overall assessment of an owner's fleet. A high level view of the standard of vessels being operated by a particular owner or manager.
HVPQ	*Harmonised Vessel Particulars Questionnaire*. The OCIMF format for vessel particulars and documents, which are of a permanent or semi-permanent nature.
Inspecting Company	The SIRE Program uses the term to refer to the company for whom the inspection is being carried out. i.e. the commissioning OCIMF member company.
Inspection	For vetting purposes, an inspection is carried out to assess the ship's apparent physical condition, and the standards of safety, operation, management, crewing, certification and equipment maintenance.
Inspection Report	The report produced by an inspector following a ship inspection, e.g. a SIRE report.
Inspector	The individual carrying out the ship inspection. A SIRE or CDI inspector should have the appropriate accreditation for the type of vessel being inspected.
ISM Code	The International Safety Management Code. An instrument of the International Maritime Organization entitled the *'International Management Code for the Safety of Ships and for Pollution Prevention'*. The Code is a brief set of general guidelines describing what shipowners must undertake in order to implement a safety management system (SMS) both on board their ships and in their organisations ashore.
ISPS Code	*The International Ship and Port Facility Security Code*. An instrument of the International Maritime Organization, the Code enters into force in July 2004. It is part of a series of measures to strengthen maritime security and prevent and suppress acts of terrorism against shipping.
Management Review (Owner Audit)	A review by vetting departments of a ship owner/manager's management systems to assess operational and technical competency. This may be carried out at the owner/manager's offices or the vetting department's offices.
Manager	This document uses the term manager to refer to the company which has the day to day responsibility for the technical operation of the vessel. Other phrases used for this are Technical Manager; Operator, Technical Operator. This company is not necessarily the same organisation or department which has responsibility for commercial operations, or which has ownership of the vessel.
Port State Inspection Databases	Such sources as United States Coast Guard, Equasis, Paris MOU, can be used to gather information on detentions and deficiencies.
Port State Control Inspection	An inspection of a vessel carried out by the national marine authority of the country in which the vessel is visiting.

Term	Description
ROVIQ	The Re-organised VIQ is the Inspector's Manual with the VIQ questions reorganised to follow the route that would normally be taken by an inspector.
SIRE	The OCIMF Ship Inspection Report Programme established in 1993 and revised in 1997 and 2000. The programme utilises a Uniform Inspection Procedure and a Vessel Particulars Questionnaire.
SIRE Report	An electronic conversion of the inspector's completed VIQ responses/comments, reformatted into a uniform report form.
SMS	Safety Management System. See ISM Code.
SPA	Sale and Purchase Agreement. A contract between a seller and a buyer for the sale and purchase of a LNG.
Structural Analysis (Structural Review)	Analysis of owner provided class information by naval architects, often employed in vetting departments.
Technical Operator (Technical Manager)	The owner of the ship or the organisation who has assumed the responsibility for operation of the ship from the shipowner who has agreed to take over all duties and responsibility imposed by the ISM code.
Terminal Feedback	Quality, operational and safety feedback from terminal operators to their principals on vessels which have called at that terminal.
Time Charter (Period Charter)	The chartering of a vessel for a fixed period of time with the vessel delivering and re-delivering at agreed dates and at agreed zones or places though usually with an option to the charterer to extend the period of charter. It is really a contract for the services of vessel and crew for a period of time with the owner insuring the vessel and maintaining the vessel in good condition and in class for the period of the charter. The charterer can order the vessel to trade world-wide (subject to any agreed exclusions) but pays for bunkers, port costs, towage, pilotage etc.
Vessel History	Changes of ownership, manager, flag, and class may be recorded by vetting departments. This is one of the elements used in assessing marine risk.
Vetting (Ship Quality Assurance)	The overall process of managing marine risk, utilising tools and processes to provide information on vessels and companies, which are being considered for business. Such tools may include inspections, inspection reports, management reviews, structural reviews, databases, marine experience and expertise, port state records and casualty data.
VIQ	*Vessel Inspection Questionnaire for Bulk Oil, Chemical Tankers and Gas Carriers*. The OCIMF document which an inspector uses under the SIRE programme.
WebSERM (SERM)	SIRE Enhanced Report Manager. The OCIMF software used to manage the storing, uploading and downloading of electronic SIRE Reports and HVPQ's

First Edition 2004

© The Society of International Gas Tanker and Terminal Operators Ltd

ISBN13: 978 1 85609 286 9

ISBN 10: 1 85609 286 0

WITHERBYS
PUBLISHING

Published by

Witherby & Company Limited

32–36 Aylesbury Street, London EC1R 0ET

Tel No. 020 7251 5341   Fax No. 020 7251 1296

International Tel No. +44 20 7251 5341   Fax No. +44 20 7251 1296

E-mail: books@witherbys.co.uk   Website: www.witherbys.com

SIGTTO The Society of International Gas Tanker and Terminal Operators is a non-profit making organisation dedicated to protect and promote the mutual interests of its members in matters related to the safe and reliable operation of gas tankers and terminals within a sound environment. The Society was founded in 1979 and was granted consultative status at IMO in November 1983. The Society has over 100 companies in membership who own or operate over 95% of the world's LNG tankers and terminals and over 55% of the world's LPG tankers and terminals.

British Library Cataloguing in Publication Data

SIGTTO
Ship Vetting and its Application to LNG
1. Title

ISBN13: 978 1 85609 286 9
ISBN 10: 1 85609 286 0

SHIP VETTING

and its

APPLICATION TO

LNG

First Edition 2004